PEDAL POWER

JAYNE WOODHOUSE

Badger Publishing Limited
Oldmedow Road,
Hardwick Industrial Estate,
King's Lynn PE30 4JJ
Telephone: 01438 791037
www.badgerlearning.co.uk

2 4 6 8 10 9 7 5 3 1

Pedal Power ISBN 978-1-78464-022-4

Publisher: Susan Ross
Senior Editor: Danny Pearson
Publishing Assistant: Claire Morgan
Designer: Fiona Grant
Series Consultant: Dee Reid

Photos: Cover Image: © PCN Photography/Alamy
Page 5: © Heritage Image Partnership Ltd/Alamy
Page 6: © pjhpix/Alamy
Page 8: © pbpgalleries/Alamy
Page 11: © Mark Beton/Capital/Alamy
Page 12: Back Page Images/REX
Page 13: Mark Pain/REX
Page 14: Andy Hooper/Associated Newsp/REX
Page 15: © epa european pressphoto agency b.v./Alamy
Page 16: FERNAND FOURCADE/SIPA/REX
Page 18: Andy Hooper/Andy Hooper Dail/REX
Page 20: Alex Livesey/Staff
Page 21: © Gaertner/Alamy
Page 23: Lobo Press
Page 24: Daniel Milchev/Contributor
Page 25: © Daryl Mulvihill/Alamy
Page 26: © Caro/Alamy
Page 27: © Yun Wang/Alamy
Page 28: © Zoonar GmbH/Alamy
Page 30: © Stephen Vincent/Alamy

Attempts to contact all copyright holders have been made.
If any omitted would care to contact Badger Learning, we will be happy to make appropriate arrangements.

Contents

Vocabulary

asthma
competitions
environment
experience

mountain
protective
travelled
velodrome

1. History of cycling

Lots of people like cycling. It is a cheap and healthy way of getting around and having fun.

Cycling helps you keep fit and is also good for the environment.

The first bicycle was made out of wood and had no pedals. It was known as a hobby horse.

You made it move by pushing your feet along the ground.

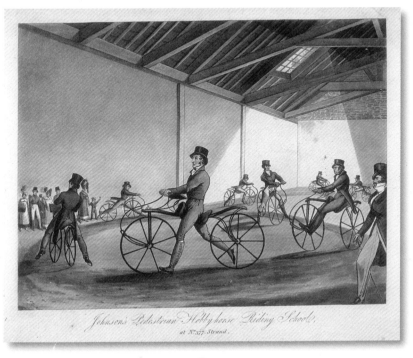

Johnson's Pedestrian Hobbyhorse Riding School,
at Nᵒ 377. Strand.

The next type of bike was called a boneshaker.

It was called this because it gave you a very rough ride.

Unlike the hobby horse it had pedals, which were fixed to the front wheels. It was heavy and hard to steer.

What is the difference between a boneshaker and a bike today?

Boneshaker	Bike today
Made of wood	**Made of metal**
Pedals turn front wheel	**Pedals turn rear wheel**
Saddle made of metal	**Saddle made of plastic shell with covering**
No brakes	**Brakes**
No tyres	**Rubber tyres**
No chain or gears	**Chain and gears**

The next style of bike was called the penny farthing.

It was invented in the early 1870s.

It was called this because it had one huge front wheel (like a big old penny) and a tiny rear wheel (like the old little coin called a farthing).

It was easier to pedal, but a very long way to fall off!

By 1900, bicycles looked a lot like they do today.

They became cheaper to buy, so many working people could afford one.

Cycling became very popular as a way of getting to work and as a hobby.

Many women enjoyed cycling. They couldn't easily cycle wearing long skirts so they wore a new style of trousers called bloomers. Some people thought bloomers were very shocking!

In 1895, Annie Londonderry became the first woman to cycle around the world.

She didn't pedal all the way. She also travelled by ship, train and carriage and did the trip in 73 days.

WOW! facts

Annie was cycling round the world for a bet of $20,000.

2. Track racing

Track cycling takes place in an indoor track called a velodrome. The track surface is made of wood.

In older veldromes the sides were not very steep but modern velodromes have very steep slopes.

A brand new velodrome was built in London for the 2012 Olympic Games.

Sir Chris Hoy won his sixth gold medal at the 2012 Olympics in the London velodrome.

"It is what I always wanted – to win gold in front of my home crowd. I can't express the feelings I'm having right now. It's just the most amazing feeling," he said.

Track bikes can go as fast as 70 kilometres per hour. Sometimes there are bad accidents.

In an accident in 1985, a pedal dug up a 33 centimetre splinter, which jabbed into the cyclist and stopped one centimetre from his heart!

The splinter had to be broken off the track surface before the cyclist could be taken to hospital.

Track racing bike

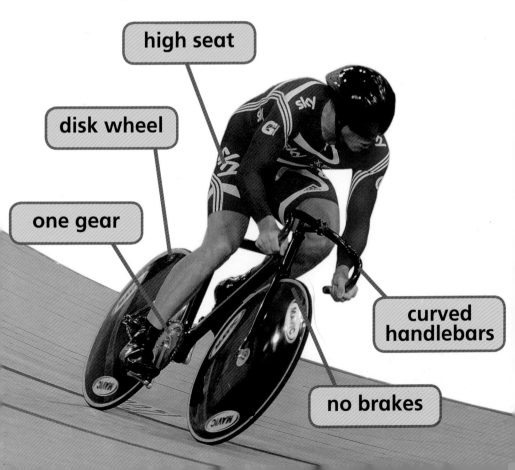

high seat

disk wheel

one gear

curved handlebars

no brakes

In 2012, Laura Trott became a double Olympic champion and world record holder and she was only 20!

Laura suffers from asthma and doctors said that cycling would help with her breathing.

She started track and road race cycling when she was eight and won her first championship when she was 12.

Paralympic athletes also take part in track races.

Blind cyclists ride on a tandem and cyclists who cannot use their legs race on handcycles.

Juan Jose Mendez from Spain lost an arm and a leg in a motorcycle accident. He rides a bike with a single handlebar and a special saddle.

3. Road racing

The world's biggest road race is the Tour de France.

It takes place every year in France and the nearby countries. In 2014, Le Tour started in the UK.

The Tour de France lasts for three weeks and covers around 3500 kilometres. The hardest stages are the climbs through the mountains.

Guide to Tour de France jersey colours:

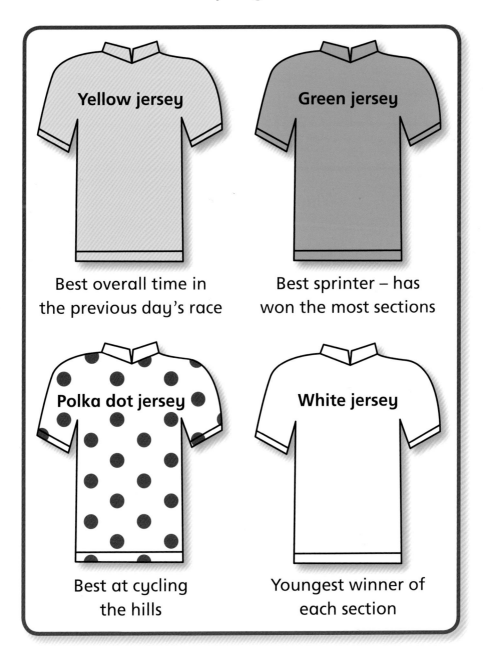

Yellow jersey

Best overall time in the previous day's race

Green jersey

Best sprinter – has won the most sections

Polka dot jersey

Best at cycling the hills

White jersey

Youngest winner of each section

In 2012, Sir Bradley Wiggins became the first Briton to win the Tour de France. He has also won seven Olympic medals.

Nicknames for Sir Bradley Wiggins:

Country	Nickname	Reason
England	Wiggo	short for Wiggins
France	'Le Gentleman'	he warned other cyclists about tacks on the road
Holland	'The banana with the sideburns'	wears the yellow jersey/has long sideburns

4. BMX

BMX stands for Bicycle Motocross. Most BMX races are held off-road, on dirt tracks with jumps. The riders wear full face helmets and protective clothes.

Top BMX racers need:

- superb bike control

- quick reactions

- nerves of steel

Races last less than a minute!

When he was seven years old,
Sir Chris Hoy was a BMX racer.
His first bike cost £5 from a jumble sale.

There is an Olympic standard track at the National BMX Centre in Manchester.

This indoor track has an eight metre high start ramp.

The top British BMX cyclist is Shanaze Reade. She races on the pro scene in America to get more racing experience before the next Olympics!

Freestyle BMX is an extreme sport.

There are five types of competition:
- street   - park   - vert   - trails   - flatland

BMX riders perform amazing tricks and stunts.

WARNING! Do not try this at home!

Can you match the BMX trick to the right description? Answers below.

TRICK	DESCRIPTION
1. Bunnyhop	A. Pedal fast while in mid-air
2. Can-can	B. Take one hand off the bars and grab the seat
3. Back flip	C. Lift both wheels off the ground
4. Toboggan	D. Turn over backwards
5. ET	E. Bring one foot over to the other side of the bike

Answers: 1:C, 2:E, 3:D, 4:B, 5:A

5. Extreme mountain biking

The Megavalanche is a death-defying cycle race in France.

Thousands of mountain bikers race 30 kilometres down a steep mountain, which is covered in snow.

The fastest riders can get down the mountain in under an hour. To take part in this race you need to be very fit and strong.

Some cyclists like to take part in extreme mountain biking competitions.

In Utah in the USA, cyclists speed down narrow ridges in a rocky canyon then take off to jump 22 metres across the canyon floor.

6. Around the world

In some parts of the world cycling is very popular.

In Holland there are cycle paths everywhere, and cars are not allowed in many places. There are signs saying: 'Bike street, cars are guests.'

At some roundabouts, cars even have to wait for cyclists to go first.

China has the largest number of bicycles in the world.

In Shanghai, there are around ten million bikes. However, more and more people are now choosing to travel by car. But with 62 mile nine-day traffic jams, it might be time for people to get back on their bikes!

In India, people use cycle rickshaws as taxis.

They are a type of tricycle with special seats to carry passengers.

You pay for a ride just like a car taxi but the driver uses pedal power to get you around.

WOW! facts

You can see cycle rickshaws in London!

Bikes in art

In 2013, the Chinese artist Ai Weiwei created a modern work of art out of 3144 bicycles.

7. Bicycles of the future

Green Shadow bike

The Green Shadow bike looks really cool. It has an on-board computer to help you track your heart rate and how many miles you've cycled.

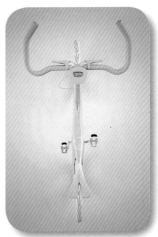

Backpack bicycle

The backpack bike folds up and fits on your back so you've got your bike with you wherever you go.

The Elf was designed in the USA and it is a cross between a car and a tricycle.

It has wheels and pedals, but when you come to a hill you can let the solar-powered motor do all the hard work!

Questions

What are three differences between a boneshaker bike and a bike today? *(page 7)*

In what year did Annie Londonderry become the first woman to cycle around the world? *(page 10)*

How many Olympic gold medals has Sir Chris Hoy won? *(page 12)*

If a cyclist is wearing a polka dot jersey in the Tour de France race, what does that mean? *(page 17)*

Where does the Megavalanche race take place? *(page 23)*

Which country has the largest number of bicycles in the world? *(page 26)*

Index